A Map of Virtue

and

Black Cat Lost

53SP 09
February, 2012

ISBN no. 978-0-9817533-9-3
Library of Congress Control no. 2012930165   ,

53rdstatepress.org

Erin Courtney

A Map of Virtue

and

Black Cat Lost

53rd State Press

Chicago, Illinois

I. UPSTAIRS FROM ERIN

I live upstairs from the playwright Erin Courtney. She is my landlady.

Seriously, she is my landlady, but that's misleading. I like to call her that though because it sounds we live in a 19th century novel. Really though I met Erin when I was cast in her witty, weird play *Demon Baby* at Clubbed Thumb many years ago. I loved this play because it was so light-hearted – the main character, Wren, receives terrifying visitations from a garden gnome. It was also, well. . . deeply sad. The sadness never overwhelmed the humor (too depressed to seduce her gay editor properly, Wren just gives up and serves him a gin tonic buck naked), but it was lurking and it felt scary. I wanted to know more.

So we became friends. And frequent collaborators. And then a year ago I moved in to the apartment on First Street with my husband, director Kip Fagan.

One of the first things we noticed is that Erin and her playwright husband Scott Adkins share our love of the sock monkey and also certain books. Most conspicuously books by or about the New York School Poets and their friends the Abstract Expressionist painters of the 1950s. This made me so happy. I was in love with the sense of camaraderie and friendly (or not) competition expemplified by these artists, and had dreamed when moving to New York that we would find a similar kind of community and maybe a loft in Soho we could rent for a few bucks a month.

And that has mostly come true for us here (minus the cheap Soho real estate). First Street is a playwrights' destination: Kate E. Ryan used to live here in our apartment, Gary Winter comes to housesit, Karinne Keithley can sometimes be found sleeping downstairs, In addition to their awesome kids Charlie and Theo, the house is often filled with 13p-ers, Mac Wellman and Erin's Brooklyn College students, and the writing groups Machiqq and Joyce Cho. And the outdoor space is home to the legendary Chochiqq Backyard Annual Theater Festival. Now I can just sneak downstairs when I have writer's block. There's always some inspiration waiting for me there. And coffee.

Erin's obvious love for artists like Kenneth Koch, Philip Guston, and Louise Bourgeois also expanded my understanding of her work. The contradiction I sensed in *Demon Baby,* of the frivolous and the dangerous uneasily co-existing, is one of the great pleasures of these artists' work, and like them, Erin delights in expressive freedom. She is willing to experiment wildly, to play with form and structure, and above all, she is unafraid to put silliness and seriousness side by side.

I. UPSTAIRS FROM ERIN

Before I began living in the apartment above Erin's, I used to visit her house for Machiqq meetings, 13P events, and parties. It looks similar to other houses on its street, and I used to forget its number, so I had to look through windows to remind myself of which was hers. Visible from the street was a large black and white painting (of a dog?) hanging on the living room wall. That's how I knew where she lived.

When we began renting the apartment, I wasn't sure how long we'd stay. I knew that I was eight months pregnant with our first child and the new place was twice as big as the shoebox we'd been living in. We were ready for change and happy to be close to Erin and her family.

My husband, son, and I lived in that apartment above Erin's for two and a half years, and then we moved to San Francisco. I was sad to give up the amazingly close proximity to Erin and her world: the backyard theater festival she organized with her husband Scott every year below what had been our back windows; the many unusual, unusually textured objects placed on mantles and tables and windowsills throughout her home; the bins of beautifully tactile toys her boys had outgrown – which my small boy loved; and the provocative pieces of art, one of which used to guide me to her home.

When I visited New York this past year, I went to Erin's house, this time to participate in a 13P documentary. The windows were blacked out, and there were lights, cameras, and playwrights scattered everywhere. Erin looked happy to be sharing her space, temporarily transformed as it was. The playwright Heidi Schreck lives upstairs now with her husband, Kip Fagan. What was our bedroom is now Heidi and Kip's living room, and vice versa. Some kind of symmetry.

II. ITS INTERIOR

Black Cat Lost could not be more different from *Demon Baby* on the surface — its narrative structure is fragmented, the characters' identities unfixed, its subject, death: specifically the death of a beloved whose absence simply cannot be understood much less accepted. Sadness is usurped here by raw grief, ugly and incomprehensible. And yet somehow the piece is still playful, still funny! There are jokes and dances and whimsical poetry, reminiscent of Kenneth Koch.

Koch said he was inspired by painters like Picasso and Max Ernst who have "the courage to do something stunning, strong, starkly dramatic and beautiful that didn't necessarily make any sense." When we first started rehearsing this play, with Erin's great collaborator Ken Rus Schmoll, it occurred to me that if *Demon Baby* was about a painter dealing with her own existential panic, *Black Cat Lost* was one of Wren/Erin's paintings. This wild meditation on mortality opens up a kind of psychic space in which we are allowed to reflect on and contend with and even make light of truths that defy sense.

> *A fine mahogany box,*
> *A ruby inside, inside*
> *the ruby a light — and*
> *finally the utter*
> *disbelief.*
>
> *Yeah. It's hard to believe.*
>
> *Absolutely. Difficult.*
> *Impossible.*
>
> *I want to become an occupational therapist.*
>
> *What is that exactly?*
>
> *I don't know but I intend to find out.*

In performance this play was funny and haunting. Ken had Birgit Huppuch, Mike Iveson and me perform the ritual lament full on, even though we weren't even sure what that meant. We just let ourselves make primal sounds that seemed like they would be appropriate if were going to ritually lament. It was one of the most frightening things I've ever done onstage.

II. ITS INTERIOR

Silence.
Silence.
Silence.
Silence.
Silence.

When reading Erin's work, even casually, one must make decisions about what's happening, and for how long it's lasting. The above list of aural directives comes just after a character describes a gratitude, a relief that is "so big." Presumably, this character couldn't – or didn't want to – speak more about this feeling. How much silence is needed to embody it, or, conversely, to put it into "relief"? If one were to stage *A Map of Virtue*, how long would this part last? What would be continually silenced?

It was never alive. It's inanimate. A statue.

In this play, a small bird statue speaks. Not only does it speak, it lets us know what it thinks about its circumstances. But "it was never alive." Its presence jars our human perspective, forcing us to create a reality in which an object has a say. We consider the bird statue's needs and its journey. If we don't, we don't arrive at the play itself.

In traditional dramaturgy, characters change. They transform. They recognize, they reverse. In Erin's work, characters express their desires poetically through song and terzanelle, through direct address to the audience and through conversations with the people around them. Whether or not they actually change may not be relevant.

III. IMAGINATIVE PROMPTS OR LICENSE FOR THE READER

Here are some things you might possibly do before or after reading *Black Cat Lost*:

1. Write your own Zen death poem. Traditionally, these could be either solemn or flippant. Haiku is a good form to use. Or you could just stick to four lines. Here are two Zen death poems featured in *Black Cat Lost*:

> *Since I was born,*
> *I have to die,*
> *And so...*
> *– Keido, 1750.*

> *And if I do*
> *become a spirit –*
> *The party's over.*
> *– Koju, 1806*

2. Watch *The Cabinet of Dr. Caligari*.

3. Spend some time with Philip Guston's ghosts, or go to Dia Beacon and look at Louise Bourgeois' giant spider.

4. Make the favorite food of a person you love who has died, and think about them while eating it.

5. Read a Kenneth Koch poem, perhaps "The Magic of Numbers."

6. Invite some people over to turn out all the lights and tell ghost stories or read Poe or Henry James or Edith Wharton ("Bewitched") out loud.

7. Go dancing.

Heidi Schreck

III. IMAGINATIVE PROMPTS OR LICENSE FOR THE READER

Here are some things you might possibly do before or after reading *A Map of Virtue*:

1. Consider symmetry. Maybe look at David Wade's book *Symmetry: The Ordering Principle*. Here's something: almost all animals are symmetrical, but sponges are not.

2. Put on a large bird mask and see if it gains you entrance.

3. Imagine holding a five-gallon industrial bucket full of water in your hand "for a long time." (Decide how long that is.) (Imagine keeping your body still.)

4. Drive to the Catskills and don't go to sleep, so there can be no middle of the night.

Kate E. Ryan

A Map of Virtue

CHARACTERS

Bird Statue – our guide through the story

Sarah
Mark

Nate – married to Sarah
Victor – Mark's boyfriend

June – dresses like a headmistress
Ray – dresses like a headmaster

PARTS

One – Curiosity
Two – Loyalty
Three – Empathy
Four – Honesty
Five – Integrity
Six – Love
Seven – Intuition

Middle of the Night – when bad things sometimes happen

Seven – Intuition
Six – Love
Five – Integrity
Four – Honesty
Three – Empathy
Two – Loyalty
One – Curiosity

"In addition symmetry principles are characterized by a quietude, a stillness that is somehow beyond the bustling world; yet in one way or another, they are almost always involved with transformation or disturbance, or movement."
— David Wade, *Symmetry: the Ordering Principle*.

SCENE ONE

Sarah and Mark are both sitting in chairs.
They are in different rooms so they do not hear each other.
They are being interviewed for a documentary film.
It should feel like their interviews have been edited together.

BIRD STATUE: Part One: Curiosity

SARAH: He seemed so kind to me. Gentle. I saw him in a diner. I was sitting in a booth near a window.

MARK: I was sitting at the counter. I was drinking tea and water without ice.

SARAH: My coffee cup was neatly placed between my two hands. I stared straight ahead, trying to keep my face relaxed. He stared at me from a bar stool at the counter.

MARK: I noticed her sitting there because she had two birds tattooed on her chest. They were symmetrical and her hands were symmetrically placed on either side of her cup. I love symmetry so I was drawn to her. She was very still and so I kept looking right at her, patiently, because she didn't mind me looking at her. She was there and I was there and for a long time there was no movement in the diner. Until the sounds of birds.

SARAH: Suddenly, there was the sound of birds. Seemed like a thousand birds — everywhere — it was just like that Hitchcock movie but it wasn't a movie, it was happening and it was really frightening. I felt frightened. I decided to hide in the bathroom of the diner. I waited there until I could not hear the birds anymore. When I came out, the man was gone. I remembered he had a notebook. I wondered what was in the notebook.

MARK: Thousands of birds. Frightening. Now, I happen to carry a small bird statue in my pocket and she had the bird tattoos and suddenly this swarm of birds was surrounding us. Some kind of omen, I thought, an omen for sure. She ran to the bathroom. The windows were darkened by the birds, the shadows of the birds, and then I saw my bus. So I ran for it and the bus driver who never looks surprised looked horrified by the birds and he said "Jesus, I fucking hate birds" just as one of them slammed into the windshield.

SARAH: I thought about him all the time and how his face looked young and smooth but his hands were wrinkled and old.

MARK: I think about what she did in the bathroom. Did she sit on the toilet? Stand over the sink? Did she cover her head?

SARAH: I don't usually go to that diner. I usually go to the bar next door because of the mixed nuts. But that bar had recently been bought by a new owner so they didn't have the nuts anymore.

MARK: About two years later, I am on vacation in Ireland. I am in a very small town called Ballybunion and I am walking along this path right at the edge of a cliff that overlooks the sea. I see a bench and I go to sit on the bench and there is the woman from the diner.

SARAH: I can see that he recognizes me and I recognize him but it's as though we have taken a vow of silence and so we don't speak and it's not strange that we don't speak. I even put my hand on top of his hand but we don't look at each other. We look at the ocean.

MARK: I thought to myself, this is the moment to finally get rid of that bird.

SARAH: Eventually, he gets up and he puts this very tiny bird statue on the bench next to me and he walks away. I sit for a while then I walk away in the opposite direction. Then I went back and put the very tiny bird statue in my pocket.

BIRD STATUE: I am the very tiny bird statue.

MARK: When I moved to Africa, I began to write letters to her. Of course, I didn't know her name or her address so I could not send them. But I found myself searching my memory for details. The blemish on her cheek, her short finger nails, and then I made up a story for her. A story about her childhood, her family, her career, her eating habits, what kind of the authors she likes to read – Dostoevsky! Dostoevsky is her absolute favorite! Well, according to my version of her.

SARAH: When I got back home, I began to incessantly draw that bird! Sometimes when I was on the phone, I would look down and realize that I had doodled it. And of course, I wish I had spoken with him. Asked him his name. Asked him why he liked birds. Asked him if he had been afraid that day in the diner. Asked him why it felt okay to touch his hand in silence. But oddly, I did not care to imagine his day job, or if he's married, or if he has children.

I did wonder about what he dreams about at night. For some reason, I often tried to imagine that. Oh, last night, I dreamt that I was trapped in some sort of strange school or retreat and we were supposed to have taken a vow of silence but all of these people were talking and that was making me really angry and I started swearing and then I called my sister and told her that I had taken this vow of silence and so I couldn't talk to her. So she panics and she sends her husband – with the police! – to come and get me and I was mad but then it turned out that the evil headmistress had poured gasoline on some of the children, was suffocating some of the children. This was all happening live and on TV at the same time. But then there was hope, a group of children had found an escape tunnel and they were making their way out. Well, it's obvious what I am trying to work out in that one. Right?

MARK: When I was a boy, I was sent to boarding school in Illinois. The headmaster handpicked a few of us – the ones he could tell that he could manipulate –and he had us meet in his library for late night study groups – but instead of studying he had us perform sexual acts on each other while he watched and masturbated. I was 12. It was a very confusing time.

His study was filled with bird statues of all sizes, from all around the world. One day, I put the smallest bird statue in my pocket. I had never stolen anything in my life but I stole it and I ALWAYS carried it with me until that day in Ireland. That little bird was looking over its shoulder. Its beak, up in the air, its head twisted up and back, looking for danger. A Meadowlark.

BIRD STATUE: I am not a meadowlark. I am a statue of a meadowlark. I have had three owners: the headmaster, Mark, and Sarah. That is, if a thing can be owned.

SARAH: When I got back from Ireland, I decided to go to art school.

I painted that bird and I drew that bird and I began to sell the paintings.

And I began to make a lot of money!

And my friends were freaked out

because I had never expressed an interest in being an artist before,

And it happened so fast, and because some of my friends were struggling painters, well, let's just say, I'm not friends with them anymore.

MARK: I had come back from Africa and I was feeling pretty weird. Intense culture shock, you know? And I walked by an art gallery and there in the window was a giant painting of my bird. I went into the gallery but no one was there. I picked up the bio of the artist. And there was her photo. She was smiling.

I know it was wrong what I did, but I took my Swiss army knife out of my pocket and before I could talk myself out of it,
I slashed the big red painting.

That was my bird.
I had left it in Ireland and she had stolen it.
I've never done anything like that, before or since.
It was so violent.

I slashed her painting. And I ran and ran until I couldn't run anymore.
And then I had to figure out how to get back home because I had run into a neighborhood that I did not recognize.

SCENE TWO

Sarah and Nate are at home.

BIRD STATUE: Part Two: Loyalty

SARAH: Some asshole slashed my painting.

NATE: What? No!

SARAH: Yeah.

NATE: Which painting?

SARAH: The one in the window. The red one.

NATE: I loved that one.

SARAH: Me too.

NATE: What kind of a person would do that?

SARAH: Some kind of sick bastard.

NATE: How could that even happen?

SARAH: The intern went out for coffee. They want me to watch the tapes to see if it's somebody I know.

NATE: What if it is someone you know?

SARAH: I hope not. I hope it's a stranger. Some random fucked up kid. You know?

NATE: Maybe its someone... who hates birds?

SARAH: Don't make jokes. It's probably someone who hates me. Right?

Sarah and Nate watch the security tape. She recognizes Mark.
She winces as he slashes at her painting.

NATE: Do you know him?

Long Pause.

SARAH: No.

NATE: Are you sure?

SARAH: Yes.

NATE: Are you okay?

SARAH: It's just a painting. It's just a thing.

20

SCENE THREE

As the bird narrates this scene, we also see the scene happen on stage.

BIRD STATUE: Part Three: Empathy

Sarah and Mark see each other on a busy city street.
They stop cold and stare, like two wild animals.

He thinks to say "I'm Sorry" but he knows it's not enough.
And he is not sure that he is sorry.
She wants to rip his eyes out and then she wants to smother him with kisses.
Is there a truce?
There might be a truce.

Mark's boyfriend, Victor, arrives and looks curiously into Mark's face.
Mark smiles and reaches out for his boyfriend's hand.
Mark and Victor walk past Sarah.

Sarah looks down at her coffee as they pass.
She sort of smiles.

Sort of.

SCENE FOUR

At a zoo in the aviary.

Mark and Sarah are both looking at the birds for a long time before they speak.

BIRD STATUE: Part Four: Honesty

MARK *(with some guilt, but also curiosity)*: Are you painting still?

SARAH: No.

MARK: Do you miss it?

SARAH: No.

> *Pause.*

I am writing very short stories.

34 syllables long.

MARK: Like a haiku. No, a haiku is 5-7-5. That's 17 syllables.

SARAH: Like two haikus.

Without the line breaks.

> *Pause.*

MARK: What are they about?

> *Sarah takes a deep breath. She doesn't really want to say but she decides she owes to him.*

SARAH: They are about a man and a bird, and a woman and a bird. The man and the woman are twenty something and they are also forty something and seventy something all at the same time. They are young and childless and they are old and parentless, all at the same time.

MARK: What color is the bird?

In the story?

SARAH: Black.

MARK: It's a meadowlark.

SARAH: I don't know. It's not alive.

MARK: It's dead?

SARAH: No. I mean it was never alive. It's inanimate. A statue.

    Pause. They both look at the birds that are flying about and whistling.

MARK *(pointing to a bird in a tree)*: That's a swallow. You can tell by its call.

    "Poor Sam Peabody, Peabody, Peabody."

SARAH: You know a lot about birds.

MARK: Unfortunately.

SARAH: I thought you loved birds!

    That's what I imagined about you.

MARK: I hate birds.

    Pause

    Your tattoos on your chest are swallows.

SARAH: I always thought they were blue birds.

MARK: Well, they're drawn with blue ink, but they're swallows. See? Look?

SARAH: I have a hard time remembering the names of things.

    I remember shapes and textures but...

MARK: Sailors get two swallows on their chest after they've been at sea for a long time. They get them to mark the fact that they made it home.

SARAH: I'm sorry... well... you were really angry at me weren't you?

MARK: I was angry at that bird because I was ready to let him go.

    I didn't want to ever see it again. You brought it back.

BIRD STATUE: Mark, I am in her pocket right now! Can you see the familiar shape? I'm right there!

MARK: I wanted to throw that bird in to the sea.

SARAH: That's strange because I almost threw him into the sea.

BIRD STATUE: I wanted to go into the sea!

    I wanted to feel the water.

    I wanted to sink to the very bottom or to be carried on a current.

    A woman carved me out of a stone.

    She sold little stone animals; turtles, birds, horses, on a table on the side of highway in New Mexico.

A boy bought me with his own money while on a cross-country road trip with his parents. He whispered to me during that long trip about all the ways he was planning to run away. When he got older, he used to tell me all the ways he was planning to kill his father, with poison, with rocks, with a gun, with a pillow. But he never did do that. No.

As he grew up, he bought more and more birds. Fossils, skeletons, eggs, sculptures from wood, bronze, terra cotta, some birds that had once been alive and now were stuffed. He became a headmaster and he ran a school and I and all the other birds lined the shelves and tables and desks of his office.

The headmaster, who had once been a boy, also liked to write Terzanelles. And he would recite them for hours on end, walking in circles in his room. The lines of the poem, repeating, he needed to repeat himself.

Some nights, he would bring a group of boys into the room. It was strange, the noises they made. The contortions their bodies got into as they jerk into some kind of position, grunting, sweating, jerk jerk jerking and then a release, a clean up, a shame, a sadness, and then the next attempt at sucking, reaching, grabbing, maneuvering inside.

Mark stole me and always carried me in his pocket, smelly, dark and always moving. His fingers working over my surface, fondling or pinching, enveloping.

And for one moment, he left me on a beautiful cliff over looking the sea. It was so beautiful. But then Sarah took me and I went back into pockets and nightstand drawers and bottom of purses with crumbs and old receipts and change.

SCENE FIVE

At Sarah and Nate's house.

BIRD STATUE: Part Five: Integrity

SARAH: I am having my tattoos removed.

NATE: Don't do that.

SARAH: I already went to my first session and it hurt like a motherfucker. It hurt way more then getting the tattoo.

NATE: Let me see.

He peeks under the bandages.

Oh, sweetie, that looks like it really hurts.

SARAH: It does.

He gives her a gentle hug.

NATE: Why? I didn't know you wanted to get rid of them.

SARAH: It turns out they are swallows.

NATE: Is there something wrong with swallows?

SARAH: No.

Silence.

Do you know why I picked these birds?

Because I saw a picture in a magazine.

A beautiful woman wearing a blue evening gown.

Her hair swept up and two bright, blue birds on her chest.

NATE: I remember that picture.

You had it tucked into your mirror

for a long time

and after you stared at it for a long time

you went and got that tattoo

and I was like, those are sexy.

SARAH: I know. They are. They were. But I didn't earn them.

NATE: Since when do you have to earn a tattoo?

SARAH: I just feel like I stole them. That's all.

NATE: Oh, you paid for them. I was there. You picked a great artist, you picked a great image in a great spot and...

SARAH: I just want to start over.

NATE: Uh-huh.

SARAH: It's not symbolic, Nate! It doesn't mean anything. I just want to be a blank slate.

NATE: Oh-kay.

SARAH: It doesn't mean anything.

It doesn't mean a thing.

SCENE SIX

At a cocktail party, Mark, Sarah, and Nate are standing together. A stranger, named June, is standing near them listening. June is wearing an outfit that somehow suggests "Headmistress". June is very attractive.

BIRD STATUE: Part Six: Love

NATE *(talking to Mark)*: When I met Sarah, she was at a friend's party.

It was a lot like this party except it was a costume party. She had this circle of people around her and everyone was smiling. She was telling some story and her story had everybody laughing. I was standing across the room so I didn't know that the reason they were all laughing was because she had just told a story about this time in college when she crapped in her pants.

I just saw the laughing and I saw her beautiful neck and she seemed giddy.

It was a costume party, so she was dressed up like a 1970's housewife. She had on this polyester pantsuit – purple I think, and a cheap wig and giant sunglasses. I come over (I was dressed like a big banana) and she offers me a pig in a blanket from her tray and she says to me "Have you ever crapped in your pants?"
So, she kind of freaked me out.

(to Mark) How do you two know each other?

MARK: We just keep bumping into each other, every few years.

In a diner,

in Ireland,

at a zoo.

SARAH *(to Nate)*: That's not true.

MARK: It is.

SARAH *(to Nate)*: No, the part about how WE met. I met you at a bonfire at the beach. And it was very quiet and we held hands.

NATE: That was the second time we met. And we walked home on that country road that was busy though, it had a fair amount of traffic, and we saw that big, wet dog running down the middle of the road.

MARK: Did it get hit?

SARAH: No, I think it was running towards home. That's how it seemed to me.

JUNE: Do you guys wanna check out this other party? I can drive us.

SCENE SEVEN

Mark, Sarah, and Nate are in the back of a van.

Nate is asleep, his head resting on Sarah's shoulder.

June is driving.

She keeps her eyes on the road but she speaks to Sarah and Mark in a loud voice so they can hear her.

BIRD STATUE: Part Seven: Intuition

JUNE: You are going to love it! And in the morning we can watch the sunrise and do Yoga!

SARAH: I just started doing Yoga. I'm not good at it but it's helping me be in my body.

MARK: I know what you mean! I am so rarely in my body.

(to June) So how long have you lived outside the city?

JUNE: Oh! A few years. I just got so sick of the city and I wanted the peace and quiet of nature. You have to build a community though or else you get lonely.

SARAH: That's why you invited us out!

JUNE: Exactly!

MARK *(to Sarah)*: I'm so glad we became friends. I mean the kind of friends that actually have conversations in real life. You know I created a fictional version of you.

SARAH: Ooooh. What was my fictional version like?

MARK: You were a single mother.

SARAH: What was it about me that made you think "single mother"?

MARK: Well, the diner was right across the street from a school. And it was 2:30 in the afternoon so I thought, her daughter goes to that school and she likes to spend 30 minutes in quiet before she has to go be the "mother" so soon, because 3:00 comes so soon, and then you have to be the "mother" again.

SARAH: And what's my daughter's name?

MARK: Maple.

SARAH: Like the syrup?

MARK: Like the tree.

SARAH: Of course!

NATE *(waking up)*: Where are we?

SARAH: June is driving us to a party out in the country. Remember?

> *Sarah, Mark and Nate have all fallen asleep in the van.*
> *June is still driving.*

BIRD STATUE:

A TERZANELLE FOR A ROADTRIP

Here is a song about where we begin
And how we map the trash we leave
The headmistress is drawn to wandering

The wandering are drawn to echo's weave
The man is drawn to the ink on her skin
and how we map the trash we leave

The woman is drawn to a bird within
The husband is drawn to a pretty neck
The man is drawn to the ink on her skin

The headmaster is drawn to meadowlark's peck
The meadowlark is drawn to an old dishrag
The husband is drawn to a pretty neck

Old dishrag is drawn to apple bag
And apple bag is drawn to ants
The meadowlark is drawn to an old dishrag

And ants to spiders to webs to plants
Here is a song about where we begin
And apple bag is drawn to ants
The headmistress is drawn to wandering

The van has stopped.

June pickpockets them.

JUNE: We're here!

SCENE EIGHT

Mark, Sarah, Nate, June and Ray are in a strange house out in the woods.
There is a large bird mask on the floor next to Ray.
Everyone sits on mattresses on the floor.

BIRD STATUE: In the Middle of the Night...

SARAH: Do you have any beer? Or whiskey?

JUNE: Why do you want a beer?

SARAH: Because it tastes good?

JUNE: Because you are an alcoholic.

SARAH *(joking, sort of)*: Ha. Ha. What kind of party is this?

RAY: You can call me Ray but when I wear this bird mask then you can just call me
  YOU and you can order me around. For example, "You are ugly. You, go get me
  some soup! You, watch this fire burn. You, read me a story." Etc.

SARAH: You know what? It's late and I think we should get home. Can you give us
  a ride to a train station? Or can we walk to one?

MARK: Yeah, I got a lot to do tomorrow.

NATE: Yeah. Thanks for inviting us.

JUNE: Well, I'm actually really sleepy. I'm going to take a nap and then I'll drive
  you to the train. Why don't you all get some rest and then we'll take you to the
  train.

June and Ray leave the room.

NATE: This is not happening.

MARK: Yeah, I think we are stuck here.

SARAH: Come on! Fuck! What the fuck!

MARK: Look out the window, we are in the middle of a freakin' forest.

SARAH: This is bad. Is it like a sexual thing? Like an S and M thing?

MARK: I have no idea.

NATE: Well I'm gonna call a car service. It's gonna cost a fortune to get a car back
  to the city.

SARAH (overlapping): Do they even have car services out here?

MARK: They do, but they are like just some guy and his car.

NATE: Where's my phone?

> They all check their pockets for wallets and phones.
> They find nothing in their pockets.

SARAH: They took our shit!

MARK: Fuck!

> Mark tries the door.
> It's locked.
> He tries another door. It leads to a small bathroom with no windows.

NATE: Shit. Shit.

SARAH (scared): Oh. This is actually really bad.

> Mark looks out the window into the big backyard.
> Ray is out in the big backyard.

NATE (rattling the windows): Hey, hey asshole, give us our fucking shit back! Jesus. He's gardening! What?

MARK: They aren't just gonna give it back to us.

SARAH: What are we going to do?

NATE: We have to get out of here and flag down a car.

SARAH: What if they have guns?

MARK: Look. We haven't seen any weapons.

SARAH: That doesn't mean they don't have them.

NATE: But they might not have any.

SARAH: But they might have some.

MARK: Let's calm down. We are going to get out of here. There are three of us and two of them.

> They look out the window.

SARAH: Oh.

NATE: What?

SARAH: Oh no.

NATE: What?!

SARAH: Ray is cleaning a shotgun.

NATE: Oh.

MARK: Oh.

SARAH: Oh.

> *They all sit back down.*
> *Lights go out.*
> *Later.*

SARAH: This is a creaky old house, little movements sound like giant bangs in here.

MARK: I don't remember what I was dreaming. Do you?

NATE: No.

MARK: I was hoping a dream would be fresh on my mind.

SARAH: Me too. I am starting to feel queasy.

MARK: You'll get...

SARAH: I'm not used to being up in the middle of night. I'm not a night person.

NATE: It is almost morning actually.

SARAH: But not really.

NATE: No, not really.

SARAH: Do you think they have food hidden in this room somewhere?

NATE: Don't do it.

SARAH: Why not?

MARK: It will make too much noise.

SARAH: I don't think they care if we make noise.

Cheese. I wish I could eat some cheese.

> *Sarah begins looking around the room. There are a few boxes and she looks in them.*

MARK: I think I saw a piece of cheese.

    Where did I see it?

Mark also begins looking around the room.

NATE: You must have dreamt the cheese. Have some more soup. It will help you sleep.

SARAH: It's not soup. It's warm water.

NATE: At least we have water.

In one of the boxes, Sarah finds a folded stack of children's clothes.
She holds up a small pink t-shirt.

She finds a child's ball.
She bounces it.
She bounces the ball many, many times.

NATE: Stop it.

She stops.
Ray, in another part of the house, picks up his ukulele and works on a song he has been writing.

RAY *(singing and playing ukulele)*:

      You like to hold this thing
      Inside your fist
      Your fist protects compactly
      Your fist protects itself.

      The axe is a fractal repeating
      The nutshell might be dead and over with
      I think it used to protect the seeds
      It's comforting that
      I still got the goods.

      You like to hold this thing
      Inside your fist
      Your fist protects compactly

Your fist protects itself.
The axe is a fractal repeating.

The nutshell might be dead and over with
I think it used to protect the seeds
It's comforting that
I still got the goods.

I still got the goods.
I still got the goods.
I still got the goods.

Lights go out.
When the lights come back up in the house, there are black out drapes that have been hammered into the window frames.

SARAH: I wonder what day it is?

MARK: I can't tell when it's night or when it's day anymore.

NATE: I think it's Monday.
 She took us on Saturday Night,
 and I think today is Monday.

> *Mark throws his body against door,*
> *THUD.*
> *Mark throws his body against door,*
> *THUD.*
> *Mark throws his body against door,*
> *THUD.*

> *Later.*
> *In the House.*

> *Mark is asleep.*
> *Sarah and Nate have sex, quietly.*

> *Then they sit quietly.*
> *There is a squeaking noise in the wall.*

SARAH: That squeaking in the wall is a bat. I thought it was a rat but now I think it's a bat.

> *They listen to the bat.*
> *There is the sound of the shotgun being fired outside.*
> *Bang.*
> *Bang.*
> *Bang.*

> *Later.*
> *In the house.*
> *June is back in the room with Mark, Sarah and Nate.*
> *Ray stands next to June holding the shotgun.*
> *June hands Mark a 3x5 notecard.*

JUNE: Mark, teach us these things.

MARK: I don't understand what this says.

JUNE: Understand it and then teach it to us.

You have three minutes.

You will be evaluated on your ability to get them to understand it.

> *June sets a timer.*
> *Mark tries to decode the words on the notecard.*
> *Mark cries and cries.*
> *Ray holds the shotgun.*
> *Buzzer dings.*

JUNE: Okay! Let's hear it!

MARK *(reading from notecard)*: Vla.

Baaaaahd.

Dur-en-schmite.

> *Mark gestures that they should repeat.*

Vla.

SARAH AND NATE: Vla.

MARK: Baaaahd.

SARAH AND NATE: Baaaahd.

MARK: Dur-en-schmite.

SARAH AND MARK: Dur. En. Schmite.

JUNE: But what does it mean?

   Explain the meaning to them!

MARK: I don't know.

JUNE: You are not trying!

   You are not trying at all!

MARK *(scared)*: Vla is a name?

   Vla is a person.

   Baaahd is a verb.

   Vla does an action — blaaahd.

   Dur-en-schmite is an adverb.

   It describes the action.

   No. NO.

   It is a location.

   It's a place.

   June shakes her head no.
   Ray grabs Mark and takes him out of the room.

   Lights out.
   Sarah and Nate are alone in the room.
   Sarah has ripped a small corner of the black out curtain so that she can see the yard.

SARAH: What's behind that garden? A fire pit? And a shed.

NATE: Do you see him? Can you see Mark out there?

SARAH: No, it's Ray. He's standing next to some kind of bonfire pit.

   But there is something in the firepit. What's in the fire pit?

   Nate looks through the small hole.

NATE: Wood. I think. For a fire.

SARAH: It's lumpy though.

Like a blanket.

Is it moving?

It looks like that blanket is squirming.

NATE: It's coal. It's a pile of coal.

Quiet.

I know you never loved me. I know you don't.

SARAH: Don't say that.

NATE: No. It's all right.

Lights out.

Later.

In another part of the house.

RAY *(itching his scalp)*: June? June, I think the head lice are back.

Ray picks up his ukulele and sings

> I just don't got no more
> No more
> This is the time of night for the
> Head lice
> I just don't got no more
> No more
> This is the time of night
> For creaking stairs
>
> I just got no more
> No more
> This is the time of night
> For sighing

Later.

June enters the room.

Ray brings Mark back into the room.

Sarah and Nate are relieved to see Mark.
Mark will not make eye contact with them.

June and Ray leave.

SARAH: Oh, Mark! Are you okay?

Sarah gives Mark a big hug.
Mark accepts the hug.
They hug for a long time.

NATE: What happened?

Mark will not answer that question.
Sarah and Mark and Nate lie down on their mattresses with their eyes wide open.
After a long time, Sarah stands up to look through the small rip in the curtain.

SARAH: Nate. Wake up. I think I see a person out there.

NATE: What?

SARAH: Look. Look. What is that?

Nate looks through the hole.

NATE: It looks like smoke. I think its smoke.

Sarah squeezing in to look.

SARAH: I think it's a child. In just her underwear. Mark. Come here.

Mark looks.

MARK: I can't see anything.

NATE: I think it's just the smoke. The fire's dying down.

SARAH: Look again.

Mark looks again.

MARK: It does look like, a little like, a girl.

Sarah is looking over his shoulder.

SARAH: Is she dancing in the fire?

MARK: If a child were in the fire, she would not be dancing. She would be screaming.

Nate looks again.

NATE: I think there is someone there. I think there is more than one.

It looks like children.

Or it's smoke.

June walks in with the shotgun.
Ray hammers the window drape shut.

JUNE: *(to Ray)* You, go get the buckets.

(to Mark, Nate and Sarah) Left arm. Straight out.

Mark, Nate and Sarah do as they are told.
Ray places a 5 gallon industrial bucket filled with water in each of their left hands.

JUNE: Your arm moves one bit, and I will drown you.

You drop the bucket and I will make you drown the person next to you.

They stand holding the buckets for a long time.
Their bodies hurt but they keep still.

Lights out.

A few hours later, Mark, Sarah, and Nate are staring into their soup bowls.
June and Ray are not in the room.

A man enters wearing Ray's bird mask.
There is a sound of crying from inside the mask.
The man takes off his bird mask and it is Victor!

MARK: Victor!

SCENE NINE

Victor, Sarah, Nate and Mark are driving fast in Victor's car.
They are happily speeding away in the car.

BIRD STATUE: Part Seven: Intuition

MARK: Victor! How did you find us?

VICTOR: GPS! Your phone has GPS.

I guess they forgot to turn off your phones!

NATE: Oh my God! Thank you! Thank you GPS!

SARAH: Thank you, Victor, Thank you

NATE: Thank you, Victor!

MARK: I love you!

SARAH: I love you too!

NATE: We all love you!

VICTOR: So what the fuck happened to you guys?

MARK: It was so stupid. This woman invited us to a party in the country and we went with her but she fucking kidnapped us!

SARAH: I've never been so scared in my life.

NATE: I really thought this is it. We are going to die.

MARK: How did you get in the house?

VICTOR: Well, I had this old pastry box in the car, tied with red and white string, and I carry the box and I go ring the door bell. Ding Dong. And this woman answers the door.

She says "May I help you?" I say "I have a delivery." "Who is it from?" she says.

I wanted to say "It's from the devil" but I can't think of anything else to say so I say nothing and she says she doesn't want to take the package and she slams the door. So, I walk all around the house and I see the black out drapes on the windows so I am thinking, this is not good. Something weird is going on. And I walk around to the side door and it's locked but next to the side door is this bird mask and so I have no idea WHY I do this, but I put the bird mask on and knock knock knock on the door. Finally she opens the door and says "If your head wasn't attached to your body you would lose it" and she lets me in!

BIRD STATUE:

A TERZANELLE FOR A STATUE

As meadowlark is categorized
A perching bird, her call a whistle sound
"see-you" "see-you" "see-yeer" "see- eyed"

Found on farms, they nest on ground
Their nests destroyed as hay is mowed
A perching bird, her call a whistle sound

In times of danger, meadowlarks shriek and goad
Loud rattle noises form in throat
Their nests destroyed as hay is mowed

They build new nests, all by rote
Moving forward, while looking back
Loud rattle noises form in throat

But I cannot warn of an attack
I cannot make that sound and call
Moving forward, while looking back

Because I am not alive at all
As meadowlark is categorized
I cannot make that sound and call
"see-you", "see-you", "see-yeer", "see-eyed"

SCENE TEN

> *Ray and June are in the room with the mattress on the floor.*
> *June is staring out window.*

BIRD STATUE: Part Six: Love

JUNE *(looking out a window)*: There is something not quite right with the garden. The lavender looks a little too tall on this side. You need to maintain the height.

RAY: I'm sorry I didn't notice that.

JUNE: I can't stand to look at it like that. I have a headache.

RAY: I'm sorry. Do you want an advil?

JUNE: I already took one.

RAY: You might be dehydrated.

Or hungry.

I could make some food for you.

JUNE: No. Thank you.

> *Pause.*

Do you have any family?

RAY: No. Not really.

JUNE: I came from a huge family.

RAY: Do you miss them?

JUNE: Of course not. They were terrible people.

RAY: It's dry tonight. Clear. Let me go make you a sandwich.

JUNE: No.

They will bring the police.

So you know what we need to do.

RAY: Yes.

JUNE: We've practiced it so it won't be difficult.

RAY: Yes.

Ray looks out the window, up at the stars.

Is that Orion's Belt?

JUNE: I never studied the stars.

Go get the gasoline.

RAY: I always thought that I would study them, but I never did.

JUNE: We can't always do everything.

RAY: No.

JUNE: And get the matches.

Pause.

Ray hesitates.

BIRD STATUE: He is not wearing the bird mask.

He thinks to himself.

I could NOT put it on.

Ray puts on his bird mask.

JUNE: You! Go get the gasoline.

RAY: Where is the gasoline?

JUNE: In the shed. Next to the canned goods,

and the first aid kit, and the axe.

Ray goes to get the gasoline and he sings from inside his mask.

RAY:

> The axe is a fractal repeating.
> I still got the goods.
> I still got the goods.
> I still got the goods.

SCENE ELEVEN

We see the scene as the bird statue describes it.

BIRD STATUE: Part Five: Integrity

> Ray returns carrying the gasoline.
> June and Ray look at each other for a long time.
> Ray would like to run but he has come too far to leave.
> Ray knows that she knows that he wants to run.
> June has no doubt about what is the right thing to do, but she is irritated by Ray's doubt.
> June strokes Ray's cheek to reassure him.
> June douses the mattress with gasoline.
> June successfully lights a match.
> She sort of smiles.
> Sort of.

SCENE TWELVE

Sarah, Nate, and Mark are all eating fast food.
Victor is still driving.

BIRD STATUE: Part Four: Honesty

VICTOR *(quietly)*: I thought you'd left me.

NATE *(slurping his soda)*: Okay, Wow. A hamburger never tasted so good.

SARAH *(with a burger in her mouth)*: Is that a mountain range?

MARK: You did?

VICTOR: Yeah.

SARAH: What's it called?

NATE *(reading a sign)*: Mt. Tremper.

MARK: I wouldn't leave you.

VICTOR *(softly)*: I thought it was like that time before.

MARK: Oh Victor. I'm sorry.

VICTOR: I was so mad.

   But something told me I should come find you.

   Something told me...

SARAH: So we're in the Catskills?

NATE: Hey, if we hadn't just been kidnapped this would be like a great weekend get-away.

   Shit. It's even more beautiful though since... you know... since we were kidnapped.

   Don't you think so Sarah?

   Sarah has stopped chewing.
   Sarah looks horrified.
   Sarah begins to spit out her food.

SARAH: Stop the Car.

   Stop the CAR.

   Oh God. GOD.

   Stop the freakin' car.

NATE: Are you gonna be sick?

Pull over!

VICTOR: I can't pull over here. It's not safe.

MARK: Are you okay? I think she's going to be sick.

SARAH: STOP THE CAR

STOP THE CAR

STOP THE CAR

STOP THE CAR

STOP THE CAR

STOP THE CAR

SCENE THIRTEEN

Sarah, Nate, Mark, and Victor are all being interviewed.

Sometimes they are in the same room.

Sometimes they are in different rooms.

It should feel like the interviews are edited together.

BIRD STATUE: Part Three: Empathy

SARAH: I had been trying all sorts of things in order to get IN my body. Meditation. Yoga. Chanting. I wanted to create a new rhythm and stick to it. To train my body to repeat the sounds, to cycle through the vowel sounds in order to take in the earth, So like this – you make a sound and then you say words that have that sound in it. It's about the sound inside the word.

MARK:

As a child I was abused by a man
obsessed with birds.
Hence, I became obsessed with birds
I became obsessed with this mysterious
woman obsessed with birds.

Then I destroyed her painting and
she very painfully erased her bird tattoos.
Then I was held captive by a bird man.

It's too much isn't it?

I mean how can that all happen?

SARAH:

AH: Ah, she saw
The law, raw
And odd
All the raw and odd
Songs she saw

AA: Her anger stays
Her anger says to stay
Away, no play, today
EE: I see, I see, you
Are free, I tree,
I please and tease

IH:I miss the kiss.
I miss the lick of the
Sick pickle of it.

SARAH: It wasn't working. None of it was working.

But when I saw June. I had this feeling about her. This feeling that she had figured everything out, that she had found a better way of living.

NATE: So Victor leads us out the back door and into his car!

And the gratitude

The relief

Was so big.

SARAH: So big.

> *Silence.*
>
> *Silence.*
>
> *Silence.*
>
> *Silence.*
>
> *Silence.*

SARAH: But after we had been driving for like an hour.

I thought, "but what about the children?"

And suddenly I am screaming and screaming

Stop the car.

Stop the car.

Stop!

And we stopped and we called 911,

And Victor gave them the coordinates of the house.

When they got there the house was on fire. I've had to live with this.

I had seen that there were children and I left them.

In that moment when Victor came in, I forgot all about them.

MARK: I feel for her. I do.

I mean I believe that she believes that she saw them.

The smoke looked like a child dancing.

BIRD STATUE: Part Two: Loyalty

NATE: I'm not going to let her die over this.

I'm worried that her guilt will... that her guilt is... you know... going to consume her...

If they do find that there were children there,

Well if that turns out to be true, then it still won't have been her fault.

She didn't light the match,

you know.

She didn't kidnap those kids.

NATE: We were sleep deprived and they had been feeding us food with no protein.

They were brainwashing us.

SARAH: Still. We had seen the children.

You saw them too!

You said, "It looks like a girl."

MARK: "looks like" a girl.

It looked like a girl but it wasn't a girl.

NATE: They have not found any remains of children.

If there had been children, they would have found the remains.

They found the remains of June and Ray.

BIRD STATUE: When you are a statue, lying and telling the truth are the same thing!

Those are just sounds coming from mouths.

There is no distinction.

The only thing I really comprehend is movement and stasis, and temperature, gradations of hot and cold.

What I really wanted, all this time, what I really wanted, was to be incinerated.

To be burned alive and transformed into something new.

To experience energy.

That's it.

Until then I am merely acted upon.

Lifted and lowered and left.

MARK: – and things come back up and pull us back and something else pushes us forward. We make some kind of association with something and this association becomes a faith. – I don't know – just sometimes our faith in something – can lead us down some paths that are bad. And each little mistake or misstep can lead us to the next one until finally it's the middle of the night out in the woods and you are on a mattress on the floor – trapped.

SARAH: But here is the thing. Couldn't there somewhere, be someone – somewhere out there – another chain of events drawing good towards you and the good is bringing more good – um consecutively? – or it follows one after the other? – what's that called?

Cumulatively?

Like somewhere, someone is following a map of virtue...

and this map is just in them...
Guiding them.
Contiguous?
I need a dictionary.
Or some water?
Could I have a glass of water?

(Mark indicates
that she has a bottle of water under her chair)

Oh! Oh!
Thank you.

(She reaches under her chair
and drinks from the bottle of water.)

Thank you.

VICTOR:
(Begins humming the
tune, ROCK OF
AGES.)

(Then he sings his
own lyrics)

Map of Virtue,
Come to me
Let me find
Myself in thee.

BIRD STATUE: I wanted to save Ray from the fire. I wanted my head to peek out from his chest, my legs to sprout from his knee caps, and my wings to grow out of the sides of his torso.

And then we could have flown out of the burning house.

MARK: We did go back.... I thought she was wrong but even after we had called the police she just kept screaming at us and so... we turned around and drove back, just to see, because she was crying so hard and yelling at us. So we did drive back, but it was too late you know.

I don't know whether or not we, it was a strange bunch of days.

We were frightened.

BIRD STATUE: But in the end, Sarah gave me what I had always wanted.

She left me on that windowsill at June and Ray's.

I was burned in the fire.

That's why I can talk to you now.

I am actually the molecules!

The ash! I finally got my wish. To be changed!

I am something else entirely now.

SARAH: Why are you pretending you didn't see it?

VICTOR: I grew up by the ocean and you learn that if a riptide takes you out, you better just conserve your energy and hope to God – or whatever you believe in – that someone notices you are gone and that that someone has the capability to come and find you and pull you out and bring you back in.

MARK: You hope someone notices you are gone.

SARAH: There were children there.

VICTOR: No. Someone else said that there were no children there.

MARK: There were no children there.

BIRD STATUE: Part One: Curiosity

VICTOR: When they disappeared, he hadn't told me about Sarah.

> None of it.
> The diner.
> Ireland.
> I had no idea that Mark had this secret friend, or enemy, or obsession.
> I had no idea that she existed and that he had slashed her painting.
>
> He needs some things to be secret.
> Or private.
> And later when he did tell me the whole thing,
> he was so really ashamed about slashing that painting.
> That was really hard for him to tell me that.
> I don't think he ever wanted me to know about that.
>
> Yeah, he had told me about the headmaster's office.
> He had told me but it's not something that he wanted to talk about too much.
> He kept that experience in a little box.
> Separate.
> But obviously he couldn't keep it separate anymore.
> As it turns out.

MARK: We were at this party and we stayed up all night and this woman who had been talking with us invited us to this other party. She said she could drive us to this other party and she drove us in this van.

NATE: A windowless van.

SARAH: Well, looking back now, I think we followed that woman, or at least I think I followed her because I had a craving for a new type of consistency. I just thought if I could just find the right pattern of my day then I could reach some type of enlightenment, or some kind of contentment. I thought maybe this woman with her cool house out in the country had discovered a new, healthier routine.

MARK: Oh. Let's see. I guess I followed the woman into the windowless van because I had been living too consistently. You know just the opposite to what you are talking about. I was finding myself horrified by the sameness of my days and it's hard for me to admit that because that includes Victor. And in the end, Victor is the one who saved us.

NATE: Why did I get into the van?

God.

I think about that a lot.

Because my wife did?

Because her new friend followed her?

Because I didn't want to get left behind?

Because I was curious.

And I did not want to get left behind.

And because she had this new mysterious friend.

MARK: Victor and I met through a mutual friend.

And I wasn't looking to be in a relationship.

I was just doing my thing.

But after two days, I just knew that he was going to be in my life for a long time. It's weird.

VICTOR: The very first time I saw him. I thought he was praying! We were at this mutual friend's BBQ, and we all sat down at these big picnic tables to eat.

And he bowed his head like this.

And I thought. Wow. This guy is religious. That's interesting.

Although, it turns out he had a migraine headache and the sun was hurting his eyes and he was trying to will his headache away.

A form of prayer but not the kind I had assumed.

Of course, an hour later the migraine had gotten much worse and he was puking into a bush. I went to help him, even though we hadn't been introduced, and he was so sick that he had no guile, you know, there was no mask. He wasn't embarrassed either, he just needed someone to help him. So I helped him get home and got him some pain killers and a wet wash cloth to put over his eyes and I turned out all his lights and closed all the curtains. And I told him I would check in on him the next day. Bring him chicken noodle soup if he wanted it.

Then I totally forgot all about him! For like three months.

It was a really busy time.

MARK: I was totally waiting for my chicken noodle soup!

VICTOR: But then we met again at that same friend's house and he was like "Where's my soup?" and we laughed and we have been together ever since. Sometimes you meet someone and that familiarity is just there right away. Like you've known them for a long time even though you haven't.

MARK: I was grateful, you know.

But it wasn't until I met him the second time that I was like, whoa.

He is really attractive.

You know, gorgeous.

VICTOR: Well, I'm glad I got to live up to my name. You have a name like Victor and it's a hard idea to live up to. That's a funny thing about names. A funny thing.

It was an incredible

endorphin rush.

Seeing him ALIVE.

She believes she saw children there.

I can only tell you about what I saw.

And all I saw was three lost and hungry adults,

sitting on mattresses.

That's it.

They did find the remains of Ray and June.

In the ashes, on the stones.

SARAH: What could make me curious again?

I'm afraid if I begin to care about something else, something other then those children, if I stop remembering them then what kind of a person does that make me? I'll have to shoot myself because I'd rather be dead then be that person.

When you put your hands together like this, you can almost feel the perfect symmetry of your body.

MARK: It looks like you are praying.

SARAH: I am just breathing.

There was a girl.

And she was dancing.

The other children watched her dance.

MARK: I think. I think you imagined that.

NATE: After all, there are some things that we can never know,

but my wife has become obsessed with the girl she believes she saw in the bonfire.

She spends her free time checking out lists of missing children to see if she can find her. To prove that she existed.

To apologize to the parents.

She remembers the girl in detail.

Brown, curly hair and about four foot one.

She had round cheeks and big bones and she liked to dance.

According to my wife.

END OF PLAY

Black Cat Lost

LEFT – a woman
CENTERED – a woman (also read MOTHER in recorded dialogue)
RIGHT – a man (also read SON in recorded dialogue)

My dog has bad dreams.
I think I know what he is dreaming.
He is dreaming about being left all alone.
No food, no water, having to shit in his own den.

Having to eat his owner.

I have to...
I'll be right...
Back...

          It's too late!

(I'll hurry.)

    You know what my son said to me the other day?

          What did he say?

    He was looking at my chin, and he said "Why do you
have a penis on your face?"

          What?

    Yeah, I think he was looking at this... But a penis?

          On your face?! It doesn't look like a
penis.

    Of course not!
He's only three...

          It doesn't look like a penis.

I'm back.
Okay.

Okay?

    Okay.
    So.

So, Gingerbread man...

There is a gingerbread man with
chocolate feet and jolly rancher hands and
nerds for eyes, ears, and mouth.

                                       Sugar frosting for hair and belt.

We eat him all up,
first the chocolate feet,
then the body,
then the arms,
and finally the head

            The next thing we want to make
            is a gingerbread house and then
            we will eat that up too.

                        On stage, there is a gingerbread house.
                        It smells wonderful. It is large enough
                        for us to sit inside of it. We will eat it
                        before the show is through.

My friend, who is an
artist, made a big gingerbread
house like that. It was in a gallery
show and the visitors to the gallery
were allowed to go into it but you were
not allowed to eat it!
It smelled wonderful.

I really wanted to eat it.

I'm going back to sleep in the dent in the wall I made last night.

Okay.

PART ONE
THE STORY OF RILKE AND PAULA

A ghost storms into the room,
messes everything up and then leaves.
Suddenly a banging.
All sorts of knocks and bangs.

I guess
that I am the ghost
of the painter and that over there is the poet
and he and I were always meant to be together,

but I was already married so,

he married my best friend, Clara.
Although he and Clara didn't last too long.

Follow... the... arrow,
follow my finger
to... the poet

I had a very, very good friend. Her
name was Paula.
She was a painter.
She was a great painter.

One of the best in the world.

And then she just died all of a
sudden. She was standing in her
room, 18 days after giving birth. She
said

"What a Shame!"

And she fell down, dead. An
embolism from her leg went to her
heart.

She died.

And since I was so mad at her for
dying or perhaps because she was
mad at me for being so mad at her,
because of all that she began to haunt
me. She would come into my room
and knock things about quite rudely
and glower at me.

She had been dead for eleven
months. And for all that time I was
trying to imagine that she was still
alive.

I'm not haunting him
because I'm mad,
I'm haunting him
because I want him to know
that I am dead
and I am still around
but that I am also DEAD.
He keeps trying to believe it hasn't happened
and that is the problem.
That's all.

But he is a very stubborn poet.
He is a stubborn poet and I bet
he'll get a good poem out of this, in any event.

        She blows out the candle.

        He relights it.

        She blows out the candle.

        He relights it.

Go to sleep.

        She blows out the candle.

He relights it.

Stubborn.

He, the poet, reads from his poem:

>"I have my dead, and I have let them
>go, and was amazed to see them so
>contented, so soon at home in being
>dead, so cheerful, so unlike their
>reputation. Only you return; brush
>past me, loiter, try to knock against
>something, so that the sound reveals
>your presence. Don't take from me
>what I am slowly learning. Once
>ritual lament would have been
>chanted; women would have been
>paid to beat their breasts and howl all
>night, when all is silent. Where can
>we find such customs now?"

Do em?
Come on,
Do em.
Do yer moves!

They do the Dr. Caligari dance.
In other words, they do the dance of the expressionistic
sleepwalkers.

Those are some good moves.
Some really good moves.

TITLE:
ZEN DEATH POEMS
PROZAC
SMALL CHILDREN
(can you hear this or am I just thinking it?)
SINCERITY
A CERTAIN GENTLENESS ABOUT IT
KINDNESS,
ACTUALLY

So, Zen death poems – the monks write them just before they die – sometimes it is hard to get the timing just right because sometimes you think it is your last day on earth so you write your Zen death poem – but then you do not die, so you are stuck with a death poem that is not really a death poem. And then other times you write a last poem. That means you write a poem, and then you die unexpectedly. So, it becomes a "last poem," an inadvertent death poem. Here is a last poem, written by JOWA in 1785.

Second Month:
I wear a new bamboo hat
And go home.

But here are some death poems:

I lean against
The stove and lo!
Eternity.

—Gazen, 1825

The cuckoo's voice
Is all the more intriguing
As I die.

–Kisei, 1764

Since I was born,
I have to die,
And so...

–Keido, 1750.

I fell down today.
I was crossing the street and I stepped up onto the
curb, but part of the curb was sloped up like this and I
tripped on it, and I fell very hard on the sidewalk –
kind of in slow motion, thinking I would stop myself
from falling, but I couldn't. So I sort of skidded along
the pavement and thud and some teenagers said –
"Hey, are you okay?" and I just kept pointing and
pointing at the messed up curb and saying "It was that
thing. It was that thing." And I wanted them to ac-
knowledge that it was the fault of the curb, not my
fault. But they didn't say anything.

It's the finality of it that makes it so tough.
No matter what we do, we will never walk
down this street with that person again.
I will never, ever see that person again
on this street corner.

Remember that time when you
imagined yourself tiptoeing up the
stairs while your children slept, you
tiptoed up to the kitchen in your
mind, and turned on the gas in the
oven and then you imagined putting
your head in the oven?

Then, you remembered your oven is electric.

         My oven is electric.

                Then you went and got on the
                prozac.

Good Job.

         It lights up
         As lightly as it fades:
         A firefly

                  –Chine, 1688.

Dance wearing a bowler hat.
The dance may or may not utilize jazz hands.
While they dance we hear the recorded conversation of mother and son:

SON: What's that?

MOTHER: That's a dance to ward off the evil spirits.

SON: Why are they wearing hats?

MOTHER: So the evil spirit can't sneak up on them.

SON: Oh and what's that?

MOTHER: That's a dead body. They are lifting it up into that cave.

SON: And what are those?

MOTHER: Those are bones.

SON: What's that?

MOTHER: That's a dance to ward off the evil spirits.

SON: Why are they wearing hats?

MOTHER: So the evil spirit can't sneak up on them.

SON: Oh and what's that?

MOTHER: That's a dead body. They are lifting it up into that cave.

SON: And what are those?

MOTHER: Those are bones.

Here is a description of a painting:
A skeleton with hair and a sort of
invisible cloak, grabs the long, thick
hair of a fleshy, round, naked woman.
Her hands are clasped together, not
quite in a praying formation, more of
a pleading one. Her eyes plead, her
chin upturned. She, alive, is in the
front. He, dead, is in the back. He is
seducing her and she is unsure of her
ability to NOT be seduced.

They perform a fuck you / let's party dance

And if I do
become a spirit –
The party's over.

–Koju, 1806

With girls and young women,
when there are two,
there is always one that has it more together.
She's got the shoes, the top, the hair, the accessories.
It's sexy.
It's easy.
No problem.
The other one is known as "the one who needs help."
She needs help picking out her clothes and shoes and accessories.
She must turn to the other girl for help.
She must borrow items from the other girl.
They get dressed together so that
"the one who needs help"

will be almost acceptable
in her appearance.

There is an observation booth at my son's school. You can stand behind the two-way mirror and watch the class. One day, I went into the booth at an odd time of day, at nap time. And I watched my son get his blanket and his sheet from his cubbie. And I watched him take his shoes off and lie down. And then I watched him struggle with his blanket. I never knew it before, but the blanket is too small and I watched him struggle and kick his feet around as he tried to get that blanket to cover his feet. And I thought is this what it feels like to be dead? To see all the complexities but to be unable to act. Maybe the dead just watch and don't feel the need to act. Maybe they have some deeper understanding of the struggles of the world, and they are beyond sadness and frustration.

Meanwhile, I sent my kid to school with a bigger blanket the next day.

The women do a ritual lament. It takes a long time and it is both frightening in its sincerity and deeply reassuring in its emotional depth.

PART TWO
HOW WE DIE

A large muslin wrapped package.

        What?

                That is what that is?

Yeah.

        Why?

It's for my heart.

                Uh-huh.

For when my heart goes out.

        In case your heart goes out.

No, when it goes out.

        What's inside?

                What's inside?

                A thoracotomy kit? With a sterilized scapel?

                A self-retaining retractor?

                A ratchet?

        Blood constituents.

What do you know about blood constituents?

        Nothing.

Nothing?

        I could make something up.

Go ahead.

No, I don't want to.

Why not?

Because I don't know what a blood constituent is? Is it what makes up the blood, I guess.

Diminishing platelets.

No. I don't think they are called that. I've never heard of that.

We need to learn more stuff.

I know.

Because I feel like I can't remember all of that stuff I learned in biology class. Or even philosophy class. Although, I can remember some things that I learned in that ex-patriot literature class.

What do you remember from that class?

I remember the classroom had French doors and I remember we read a book written by Graham Greene and I remember we painted a mural on the wall of the classroom. I think it was a painting of a lonely man. A skinny lonely man in a grey suit. But actually, I might just be remembering the teacher. The teacher looked like that.

I've got a charley horse.

Breathe into it.

Owwww. Owwww. SHIT. SHIT>SHIT.

                              Stop fighting it.

It's seizing up.

                              Allow yourself to recognize the pain.
                              Pay attention to the sensation.

It's passing. It's passing.

                              See!

See what?

                              You stopped fighting it and then it
                              didn't hurt so bad.

No. The pain just stopped.

                              You should practice the Schaufenster
                              Schaven.

Schau whatser haven?

                              It's German for windowshopping.

                              It means you stop to look into store
                              windows.

I do that.

              Do you have everything for the audition?

                              Yeah.

Yeah. The sides. The schedule. Water.

I've always wanted to play one of those depressed
Chekhovian Russian women.
You know the Mashas unhappily
engaged to the school teacher.
And she wears black because she is in "mourning for her life."

That explains the outfit.

Yeah. I got the outfit worked out, so far.

My favorite actor of all time had no teeth.

So, he had dentures?

No. He performed with no teeth.

Oh, come on!

No, he did.

Yeah, I saw him.
He performed Chekhov.
He was great.

Is he hard to understand?

He is…

He is…

He is…
Epiphianic.

Please.

Every word was new.

That sounds like a very bad joke!

Oh. No. It's true.

To be eaten by a wolf
and to have the wolf cut open and to
emerge whole.

The terminal event is not terminal!

Well, it's a calcification.

Calcifications.

Right. Calcifications.

You know what's missing?

Celebrations of festive joyousness.
I am sure that I have been involved in lots
of celebrations of festive joyousness
but at the moment I cannot think of any.

We marched along the sidewalk in
costumes. When we got to the
woods, they had a ceremony and men
emerged wearing deer antlers.
They danced a slow dance
and then we went inside for a party.

I used to dance all night long. Our favorite place was
called Ballroom Blitz and it was on Fairfax. One night
I wore a striped orange and black t-shirt and black
tights and high heels. And when I was standing on the
street a group of people asked me if the 1960's look
was my specialty. I said no. I think they thought I was
a hooker. But I was very proud of my outfit and I was
trying to look like Edie Sedgewick. And on some level
my attempt was very successful.

Out of the gingerbread house,
come lots and lots
of children wearing
deer antlers.
They perform a
tap dance that
makes you so happy,
you cannot stop smiling.

PART THREE
ON DEATH AND DYING BY DR. KUBLER-ROSS

This is inspired by a game.
I'll tell you the rules later.
I promise.
And you might want to play it because it is fun,
– if you can be playful.

SCENE ONE

Here is the problem with epidemics, are they based on a wish?
A naughty deed enacted by a young child.
All of this grief, shame, guilt, anger and rage,
all from the death of a farmer.

SCENE TWO

Epidemics!

      Scary.

Because everyone goes all at once.

      Large swaths of people go.

And you wish it would stop.

           But it won't.

And it's beyond our control.

      And we love! Control!

           Who doesn't?

      What's that?

A deed.

      To what?

To my house.

Why?

In case I go in the epidemic.

Who are you going to will it to?

Someone.

What if we all go in the epidemic?

Then it won't matter anymore.

A young child enters and hands the couple a piece of paper.
The couple reads the paper –
"This grief, shame, and guilt."
Young child says, "anger and rage."

Have you been walking a long time?

The girl shows her blisters on her feet.

And what did you see?

Girl draws a picture:
A man in a straw hat with x's over his eyes.

A dead farmer. You saw a dead farmer?

YES.

Girl hands him the note.

"I have a certain anger at God."

Is this your handwriting?

Girl nods yes.

Have you dipped in the well?

Girl nods yes.

> Have you swallowed the pomegranate?
> Have you cracked the
> peanut shell?
> Have you touched the
> light bulb?

That's enough with the euphemisms. She clearly has no idea what
you are saying!

> Girl: I ate the glass balloon.

> See, she knew what I meant all along!

Okay. Okay. So she's been to the emergency room.
What does that prove?

> I think it's time we sat down and took
> a good look at our society.

That's what Mr. P always said to do!

> And Mrs. A!

But not Mr. D.

> Oh no! Mr. D always wanted to avoid
> taking a good look at society.

His initial denial did lead to partial acceptance eventually.

> But he would never admit that!

No. No. It was a very internal, private sort of acceptance.

> I should not have ate that giant muffin.
> It's making me sleepy.

> You were sleepy already!

Now I am sleepier. God.

> In summary, Mrs. K was diagnosed
> with terminal liver disease. So, she

> embarked on a journey to find a faith healer and to eat only a protein free diet. Her therapist, her occupational therapist, was in utter disbelief at this approach. But Mrs. K said to Dr. A "I am not dead yet!"

And what of Mr. X?

> Well, Mr. D asked to come for a visit.

Yes?

> And Mr. X said "Not now, come later."

And then Sister I...

> Found a note – scrawled – and it said...

Agno.

> No.
> Anger and Resentment

And finally

> Reaching out
> Wishing to go
> Places.

SCENE THREE

I am always reaching out. I am wishing to go places.

> Do you find your friends greet this idea with anger and resentment?

Oh yeah!

> They are afraid to reach out and they are afraid to go places.
> So, they want you to
> stay put.

Exactly.

There is a rustling or a knock.

Not now! Come later! So, what about Mr. D?

The brother of Mr. X?

Yeah, yeah.

Oh well he's doing better you know. I
went to visit him and brought him
flowers and a little card and he
shouted at me "I am not dead yet!"
So even though
it kind of hurt my feelings, because I
took a long time picking out the
flowers and the card, I also think it is
a very good sign.

And what did Dr. G say?

Dr. G said not to get our hopes up.

Oh.

Yeah.

Geez.

Yeah.

I know but it's hard not to get our hopes up.
He's sitting up.
He's talking.
His color is coming back.

This inside of that.

What?

A jewel box.

Uhm…

          A fine mahogany box, a ruby inside,
          inside the ruby a light – and finally
          the utter disbelief.

Yeah. It's hard to believe.

          Absolutely. Difficult. Impossible.

I want to become an occupational therapist.

          What is that exactly?

I don't know but I intend to find out.

          I wanted to become a therapist
          therapist, but I thought I would get
          too caught up in my client's stories, I
          think I would be too empathetic, not
          analytical enough. Oh! And I just
          started a protein free diet.

Can your body survive without protein?

          Yeah, yeah why not?

Well, I just thought that a body needs protein to survive.

          I saw a faith healer. She told me to
          try it.

Why did you go to a faith healer? Are you sick?

          Terminal liver disease.

What?

          Yeah.

When did you find out?

          2 months ago.

And you waited this long to tell me?

I just wasn't ready to believe it myself.

Wow.

I was in denial.

Whoa.

Then came anger. I even slapped
Mrs. K.

You slapped Mrs. K?

She was bothering me! She kept saying,
"In summary," and I said to myself, if she
says in summary one more time then I
will slap her. She did and I did.
Now. Now I think I have reached a stage
of partial acceptance.

After your initial denial.

Yes.

But now, I am in denial.

Yeah, you will be for awhile.

What about Mr. D, Mrs. A and Mr. P? Have you told them?

Oh, they really, really, freaked out. They
began to study the situation intensely –
"what are the causes? Look at our
society that we could let this happen!
What are the therapeutic alternatives?"

How did you find out?

Oh. I had this pain so I went to the
emergency room, and after a string of

euphemisms, they just came right out and said the word, "terminal."

God. How do you feel? How are you doing?

I feel: anger at God. I feel upset that other people will go on living after I have gone. But then I started to read this book. It's called "The Death of a Farmer." And I thought it couldn't possibly help but it helped.

"The Death of a Farmer."

I'm gonna write that down.

I have to read that.

It helped me deal with my anger and rage and all this grief, shame and guilt.

Because of your child,

Because I do have a young child.

That you will have to leave behind.

A bad deed.

Yeah.

To leave a young child behind.

It's gonna be hard.

If I had a wish...

Yeah... one wish... what would you wish?

I'd wish to not be sick and about to die.

Of course.

But it could be worse.

How?

It could be an epidemic. And the problem with epidemics is that then the whole family goes, that the whole community can go all at once and then the memory dies and the legacy dies and there really is nothing left.

Yeah. "Death of a Farmer"

Yeah. "Death of a Farmer"

Got it.

I dreamt last night that I was making a film about a young woman painter who was in art school. This young woman painter kept a journal and every day she sketched the critique. In other words, she would draw a picture of the student painting that got the most positive critique from the teacher. And then she would write her own critique under it – "stupid", "simple", "seen it before, seen it done better", "bore, bore, bore" and "lies".

Needless to say, she soon dropped out of school but she had a small circle of friends that were very dedicated to her even though she was always fucking up and hurting people's feelings and getting into trouble with the law. They were dedicated because they saw that she could see something that they could not see. They loved her for that. She rented an apartment but she had no money, so the scene we were filming was of her friends coming over to tell her that she had better leave right away because the landlady was coming. So she stands in her cluttered bedroom-slashpainting studio and she says "What should I do?" and the friends look around the room and they can hear the footsteps of the landlady (who was actually very compassionate and idiosyncratic and had NO intentions of kicking the young woman painter OUT or pressing charges or anything). SO. The friends say HURRY, HURRY, you have to leave. She looks at her art and decides its all crap and nothing worth taking with, same with her books and scattered detritus, so she thinks I'll just take my purse and she climbs out the window and she leaves absolutely everything behind.

HEIDI SHRECK

Hi my name is Heidi Shreck and I have been playing the part of Audrey West which is a slightly fictionalized version of Erin Courtney, the playwright. In the event that I, Heidi Shreck, am unable to play the role of Audrey West a.k.a. a fictionalized version of Erin Courtney, daughter of Robert and Dorothy Courtney, born in Hermosa Beach, California in 1968, married to Scott Adkins in 1999, mother of Charlie, born in 2001, and Theo, born in 2003, and sibling to Colleen Cole, John Courtney, and Mary Burke, then another actress by the name of _____will be performing this role.

If Heidi Shreck is unavailable, then this actress should do an impersonation of me, Heidi Shreck, impersonating Erin Courtney in her thinly disguised persona of Audrey West.

I, Heidi Shreck, am taller and blonder than the author.

Another actor, may have different features entirely.

So let's continue on, with the story of the BLACK CAT.

Once upon a time there was a young child who harbored a great deal of anger at God. Why should such a young child be so angry at God?

Mr. P: Hello, my name is Mr. P. I am the young girl's uncle and I can tell you why the young girl is very angry at God because she believes that God is responsible for the loss of her Black Cat. The cat was home happily drinking her milk in a blue, porcelain dish when she saw a strange, yellow bird outside the open window and the cat ran out to chase it and the cat never returned.

Mr. H: To the girl, the bird was God and God had lured the cat away. He may or may not return to the story of the cat.

Mr. P: It turns out that I am only slightly able to accept. I'm in a stage of partial acceptance of my terminal liver disease.

Occupational Therapist (OT): Today's activity is weaving. Here is the loom. Here are some wonderful colors of yarn. Feel the different textures. Choose a color you enjoy.

Mr. P: I am not interested in weaving.

OT: It will lower your stress.

Mr. P: Did I tell you my niece lost her cat.

OT: Yes. You told me. This weaving had a great effect on Mr. X.

Mr. P: Mr. X is in denial. AND Mr. X
Is not an agno... Agnostic.

OT: Are you an agnostic?

Mr. P: Yes.

OT: So that means you don't believe in weaving.

Mr. P: I hate this activity. I hate this
game. Please can we switch. It is silly
and repetitive. I don't like these
words.

I am not dead yet!

AUDREY: He is skipping ahead.

Mr. P: Sister, I... Sister, I have a
wish.

OT: Should we take him to the emergency room?

AUDREY: In summary, they are taking a short cut.
They are skipping words that they are not interested
in.

Mr. P: Not now, come later.

HEIDI: He is reaching out. He is wishing to go places.
And that is it. And that is all.

I'm lost.
I don't know which direction to go
in. I saw the street that had my
childhood home. I mean the home
that I was born in but I didn't walk
down the block because I heard that
house had been torn down and a new
house had been built on the spot. It
was my first childhood home and

then it was Paul's home and Paul is
gone and the house is gone and my
childhood is gone. I didn't go look. I
have a picture in my head that I
would like to keep. The bumpy brick
path that led to the back patio, a
green arched doorway, the door that
led into the kitchen, the bathroom
door that stuck, the narrow hallway
upstairs that made ship-like sleeping
quarters for kids but then opened up
into a roundish room with a window
that was sort of like the ship's prow?
Is that the word?

We need some other character!
The one with terminal liver disease?
The nurse
The doctor
The patient
The child
The farmer
The poet
The painter
The dancer
The waiter

THE ARCHITECT!

Yeesss?

There is a living room with
A decanter, a fireplace, an oversized chair, an arched
doorway, picture molding, and a Persian rug.

Three wild dogs inhabit the space.
They live there!

One wears a partial hound mask.

One has a tree branch for a paw.
One has something else that indicates,
"dog."

All I can do is make lists.
And wait.

It's like the prozac has taken my brain away
and I cannot see a world.
There are no pictures in there —

I saw that in a dream, the ----- with the ---- in it.

Just lists —

Lists are so

Static (?)

A woman sits in a bed, all wrapped in a white sheet.

A woman enters, all tanned, muscled
legs and flip-flops-mini-skirt-tank
top-long-blonde-hair-breasts-that-
float — she holds her wallet behind
her back. She sways slightly as she
waits for her order. "No I didn't want
the bagel toasted. Sorry. Sorry. Can
you just slice it? Thanks." Plays with
her earring, cools down her coffee by
blowing on it. The man with her
whistles, a little whistle.

What do you want to be done to your body after you
die?

What kind of funeral do you want?

The doctor emerges and speaks...
This breakfast burrito is too hot,
a piece of egg just fell out of my mouth.

When I don't know what to do, I just want to shove food in my
mouth.

      This is where you really, really say goodbye and never
      see the person again.

            Is the person dead?

No.
Well. I don't know.
I haven't seen them.

            Well, so you may see them again? It
            may not be the very last time.

      Is that a supermodel?

Where?

      Right over there.

Cute, striped tunic.

      I don't want to write a play about death anymore.
      I dreamt I was cast in a BROADWAY MUSICAL
      but I can't sing or dance or act.
      So, I kept coming late to rehearsal although it seemed
      that the whole cast was equally miscast.
      We tried to kick in unison wearing black
      fishnet stockings and we tried to tap but we had no
      tap shoes. But it was also like Chekhov or James Joyce
      and the stage manager kept forgetting to give me the
      rehearsal times and yet I still wanted to be in this play.

      Still, I desperately wanted to keep the job and
      perform on Broadway.

Fishnet and bowler,
striped socks and beret,
boots and umbrella.

First just legs,
then their laps with items on them.

All covered over.

From a clothes catalog:
3 Ladies,
gone friend,
Audrey,
Rilke,
gone friend.

Then some voices,
some dances.
Inches up.

Dance in the middle.
Live ones move the dead ones around.

Shift them,
place them

MIRROR

CARDBOARD

(or) CURTAIN

Look and they look away.
That's all we can do.
That's why it's a list.
See?

I like the idea of classifying things,
putting things into nameable categories.
And each category is defined
and there may be sub-categories
to the main categories
and chapter titles.

And then section titles
within the chapters
but I just like the idea of
classifications.
I find that reassuring,
very reassuring.

PART FOUR
THE TIBETAN BOOK OF LIVING AND DYING

"Presence"
"Therefore"
"Impermanence"
"Wish-fulfilling jewel"

"Telling the truth"
"Losing the body"

"Finally we took the body to the place
he had chosen for the cremation"

"I find it extremely suggestive that
modern physics has shown that when
matter is investigated, it is revealed
as an ocean of energy and light"

"Our life was better having known him"

He worked in the Brooklyn Navy Yard.

He loved music.

He was a good neighbor.

His name was Amerigo

but the nuns renamed him

Henry.

One night, I heard my grandma Ida talking in her
room.
I walked into her room
and she was sitting up
in her single bed.

Her face looked just like a child's
and she had her hand dangling over the side
of her bed.

And she said,

"Oh Jenny! Feel this river. It's cold."

He was ready to go home.

"Many of those who have come near
death speak in a personal, undeniably
eloquent way of the -----, ----, -----,
and ------ of what they have
experienced."

I dreamt about him last night and he was young
and radiant and he told me that I was doing the right thing.
That I was my own boss and that I was following my heart
and that, that was the right thing to do.
I wasn't that close to him when he was alive –
so why would he come to comfort me in my dream?
He looked like an impish god.
Spikey blond hair, tan face, rounder than I remember it.

Oh! Yesterday,
a student of mine told me that he believes that death is
a transcendance. I found that to be a beautiful word
choice.
Now, follow my finger… to another poem
by someone else written for someone
else.

Throw yourself up against the
Murphy Bed – a seduction!
Take a trip out all around the
universe in the planetarium.
Even though Tom Hanks was the
narrator,
we did not like the feeling of being
sped so far out into space.

Because you and I were both born
premature
so connecting with people was
number one priority.

Once in a restaurant when I was stuck,
you said to me,
"Just write it down the way you just said it."

Once in a restaurant,
while I was wiping down the
glass table tops and
Car Wash was playing on
the jukebox, you wrote
a poem for me on a
napkin.

Once in a restaurant,
you came to say goodbye to me
and I was just too young to
understand what you were doing.

He performs the BOB FOSSE/PHILIP dance.

Oh.

Oh?

I need to practice it still.

Come on,
do yer moves,
do 'em.

It's complicated. It's me
imitating him, imitating
Sammy Davis Jr. while Michael
Jackson sings "Man in the Mirror."

I thought you rehearsed it.

I need more time.

But. That dance needs to be here.
Right now in this section.

We could sing that Carter Family Song?
"Death is Only a Dream"

EPILOGUE
THE STORY OF SISTER MARY CORITA

Sister Mary Corita says:

> "I am a school teacher.
> My job is to infiltrate
> The masses."

Here is an example:

Makes
Meatb
Allsing

Pigeons
On the
Grass
Alas

SISTER MARY CORITA
was a nun and an artist and a teacher.
and she was a good friend to a lot of poets, actually.

I had a habit of stealing buses,
public buses,
and driving myself to wherever
I wanted to go.

I had stolen lots of buses
but in the snowstorm
I drove the stolen bus
into a drift of snow.

I was arrested at the nearest
subway station because
they had already captured
my picture from a surveillance camera
near the snow drift.

After I was arrested,
a team of very prestigious lawyers,
lots of them, maybe forty or so,
interviewed me in this
large fancy conference room.
They were trying to decide if they should take my case.

No one asked me if I stole the bus.
They asked me deeply personal
and psychological questions.
One read from a piece of paper
I had been carrying. He said
"We found this word on a piece of
paper and the word is... attempt... why did you write that
word?"

"I wrote that word because as a teacher and an artist – it's impor-
tant for my students and myself to attempt things and perhaps
sometimes to fail – but to be brave in our attempts."

The lawyer said
"Oh yes, I like that answer."

Meanwhile, I wanted to shout,
"I stole the bus!"   "I stole the bus!"   "I stole the bus!"

There was some discussion of keys and recognition
of keys and whether or not I knew how to hotwire a bus.

So what do you want it to be then?

Not guilty for reasons of anxiety and
frustration.

The white guy nods his head.
It seems like a good possibility.

I'd like to fly and see him.
Isn't that strange.

I only kissed him one time.
It was late, after a party, and
he was my brother's friend.
It was so soft and sweet that kiss.
I always liked him, because he
was always doing things other
people disapproved of, but I thought
they were fine choices.
Now, I just found out he is really sick
from some mysterious thing
and he will probably die
and I would like to go see him,
even though I haven't seen him in
fifteen years.

THE STORY OF SISTER MARY CORITA
Sister Mary Corita says:

"I have a theory (she said, and contin-
ued laughing) which doesn't work!
It's that there's nothing ugly. If you try
this out you find you block out fewer
things than if you just go around looking for what is beautiful or great." For
example, in advertising.
Advertising about Meatballs.

Makes Meatballs sing

Makes
Meatball
sing

Makes
Meat
ball sing

Makes
Meatb
All sing

       Makes
       Meatb

       All Sing

END OF PLAY

Erin Courtney's other plays include *The Service Road*, *Honey Drop*, *Alice the Magnet*, *Demon Baby*, and *Quiver and Twitch*. She has collaborated with Elizabeth Swados on *Kaspar Hauser: A Foundling's Opera* which was produced at the Flea Theater and named one of The Downtown Theater Favorites of 2009 by Tom Murrin of Paper Magazine. Her plays have been produced or developed by Clubbed Thumb, Adhesive Theater Company, The Public Theater, The Flea, The Vineyard, Playwright's Horizons, NYS&F, and Soho Rep. *Demon Baby* is published in two anthologies: *New Downtown Now*, edited by Mac Wellman and Young Jean Lee and published by University of Minnesota Press, and *Funny, Strange, Provocative: Seven Plays by Clubbed Thumb* edited by Maria Striar and Erin Detrick and published by Playscripts, Inc. She is an affiliated artist with Clubbed Thumb, a member of the Obie award winning playwright collective 13P, as well as the co-founder of the Brooklyn Writer's Space. Ms. Courtney teaches playwriting at Brooklyn College. She earned her MFA in playwriting at Brooklyn College with Mac Wellman. She co-hosts the annual CHOCHIQQ backyard theater festival with Scott Adkins.

A Map of Virtue

Thank you to Erik Ehn and Pataphysics, Mac Wellman and the Brooklyn College band of rascals, Scott Adkins, Anne Kauffman, Susan Bernfield at New Georges, Pam MacKinnon, Maria Striar, Clubbed Thumb, Matthew Maguire, the Fordham University Theater program, Antje Oegel, Karinne Keithley Syers, Chochiqq, Prelude, Sarah Krohn, the Williamstown Theater Festival, Ken Rus Schmoll, Caleb Hammons, Maria Goyanes, all the playwrights and staff of 13P, and to all the actors who have participated in the various readings of this play in backyards, living rooms, rehearsal studios and theaters.

A Map of Virtue was produced by 13P in February 2012 at the Fourth Street Theater in NYC, directed by KEN RUS SCHMOLL, sets and costumes by MARSHA GINSBERG, lighting by TYLER MICOLEAU, sound and music by DANIEL KLUGER, production stage manager was MEGAN SCHWARZ DICKERT*, casting by KELLY GILLESPIE, associate producer was RACHEL SILVERMAN.

Featuring ALEX DRAPER* as Nate, BIRGIT HUPPUCH* as the bird statue, JESSE LENAT* as Ray, ANNIE MCNAMARA* as June, HUBERT POINT-DU JOUR* as Victor, JON NORMAN SCHNEIDER* as Mark, and MARIA STRIAR* as Sarah.

* Member, Actors' Equity Association

The production was made possible in part by a grant from The MAP Fund, a program of Creative Capital supported by the Doris Duke Charitable Foundation and the Andrew W. Mellon Foundation.

Black Cat Lost

Thank you to Daniel Aukin, Sarah Benson, Mark Sitko, the ladies of Machiqq, Chochiqq, Matthew Korahais, Mac Wellman, Pavol Liska, Karinne Keithley Syers, and Scott Adkins.

Black Cat Lost was commissioned by Soho Rep and given a Studio Series presentation there in 2009. The play was directed by KEN RUS SCHMOLL, and performed by BIRGIT HUPPUCH as Left, HEIDI SCHRECK as Centered, and MIKE IVESON as Right.

Always grateful to Robert and Dorothy Courtney for everything, all the time.

Cover image by Erin Courtney
Back cover photograph by Rebecca Jane Gleason
Book design by Karinne Keithley Syers

53rd State Press publishes new writing for performance. It was founded in 2007 by Karinne Keithley, is incoporated in the state of Illinois, and is co-edited by Karinne Keithley Syers and Antje Oegel.

For more information or to order books, please visit 53rdstatepress.org.